Algernon Whitmore

Radical wisdom

Being a selection from the wise, witty and patriotic sayings of notorious

radicals

Algernon Whitmore

Radical wisdom
Being a selection from the wise, witty and patriotic sayings of notorious radicals

ISBN/EAN: 9783337276492

Printed in Europe, USA, Canada, Australia, Japan

Cover: Foto ©Andreas Hilbeck / pixelio.de

More available books at **www.hansebooks.com**

PRICE SIXPENCE.

Or Thirty-two Shillings per Hundred Copies.

RADICAL WISDOM.

BEING A SELECTION FROM THE

WISE, WITTY, AND PATRIOTIC SAYINGS

OF

NOTORIOUS RADICALS.

BY

C. ALGERNON WHITMORE.

"We are party men first and last on all questions."
Sir William Harcourt, M.P.
"At every word a reputation dies."
Rape of the Lock.

LONDON:

W. H. ALLEN & CO., 13 WATERLOO PLACE,
PALL MALL, S.W.

1880.

INTRODUCTION.

SINCE their inexplicable defeat in 1874, the leaders of the Radical party have performed the oratorical duties of an. Opposition with extraordinary diligence. So various have been the modes in which they have given expression to their views, so unceasing has been the flow of their eloquence, that some careless Englishmen may have failed to appreciate the full and perfect wisdom of their thoughts. In this pamphlet I have attempted to rescue from possible oblivion some of the more remarkable of the doctrines, sentiments, prophesies, and witticisms that are lying scattered amidst this wealth of words. It will be seen that I have by no means confined myself to extracts from speeches delivered in Parliament. Mr. Gladstone and his friends have by no means confined their eloquence within the walls of Parliament. It was by pamphlets and in the pages of the " Nineteenth

1 *

Century Review," that Mr. Gladstone explained his whole foreign policy. It was during a five minutes' wait at some wayside station, and from the window of an express train, that he expounded his most mature and profound political philosophy.

The second portion of this collection is devoted to Political Prophecies. None of these prophecies have been fulfilled ; most of them have already been proved false. They are introduced here mainly to gratify Sir W. Harcourt, and also for this reason. The charity of the Liberal leaders in mundane matters seems so heavenly, and their acquaintance with the desires of Providence seems so unaccountable, that it may well be that some timid and devout Scotch souls regard them as hardly "canny," and are fearful that a Nemesis will follow on unselfishness and spirituality more than human. I trust that this series of political prophecies will reassure such souls. At all events, it proves conclusively that in the matter of prophecy the Liberal leaders have received no supernatural gifts.

There next succeed a few selected jests. Though the Radical party has its own two jesters, it does not itself like jokes very much. And it may seem frivolous to range specimens of humour by the side of specimens of political philosophy and prophecy. My object, let me explain, is not only to excite the laughter of the world—there is a loftier

object in view. Enthusiastic Conservatives are
never weary of asserting that Liberals cannot
agree on any one subject. Behold the refutation
of the calumny ! Selected is a jest by each of
the two Radical jesters. Verily, they have this
essential quality in common. The naughty drollery
of each depends upon alliteration, and upon alliteration alone. On the vexed question, therefore, of
what is humour, the Radical jesters have arrived
at an identical conclusion, and their unanimity is
truly ridiculous.

At the end of the pamphlet, lest malignant
Tories should sneeringly exclaim, "Oh! of course.
the Radicals can say clever things ; but where
are their deeds?" I have shown concisely how
the Radicals have, in fact and by deeds, vigorously
and not ineffectually hampered every effort of the
selfish Tories to maintain the honour and interests
of these small islands, and to preserve the peace
of Europe. It would be a grievous mistake to
imagine that the only weapon of the Radicals has
been an isolated phrase.

In several instances the wisdom of modern Radicals has been illustrated by a comparison of it
with what Liberals of an earlier period and less
enlightened men of the present time have said on
the same subject. How prodigious is the contrast !
What immense strides have been made in the
science of political philosophy in the last few
years! Poor Burke! mistaken Chatham! how

false were your conceptions—how injurious your practice! It is but within the last few years that (thanks be to thee, beautiful Birmingham) we have begun to emancipate ourselves from the debasing influence of that vulgar passion—Patriotism.

Ancient Radicals may resent the introduction of some sayings of Lord Derby. In truth, I hesitated long before admitting him into the company of Liberal worthies. I could not but remember the virulent abuse that was showered upon him by the Radical Press and by Radical speakers in 1876 and 1877. But an article in the " Spectator " finally dispelled my doubts. In that article a speech of Lord Derby's is characterised as " clear-cut." What this term may mean I know not ; but every reverential reader of the " Spectator " will agree that it is used as an epithet of supreme praise, and conferred only on the very best of good Radicals. Lord Derby, therefore, has been formally recognised by the highest authority as a good Radical.

It is disappointing that the titular chiefs of the Opposition should contribute so few examples of novel wisdom. A careful study of Lord Granville's speeches has persuaded me that he has really said nothing which any sensible Liberal of the first fifty years of this century might not have said ; and this, alas! is true of Lord Hartington's observations on Foreign Policy; though it is but fair to point out that on domestic ques-

tions he has said some notable sayings, which no
sensible Liberal would ever have said before the
Gladstonian era.

It is also a subject for regret that so many of
the best sayings of our Radicals should have been
suggested by Foreign Affairs. Would that they
could have devoted their thoughts to larger and
more grateful topics, such as Local Option, Vivi-
section, Anti-Vaccination, and the repeal of the
Contagious Diseases Acts. Would that they
could have set class against class, have reviled the
tyranny of the Church, and sung of the wrongs
of gentle Dissent. Alas! they could not; for,
Lord Beaconsfield in 1876 decided to re-open the
Eastern Question, and since then has gratuitously
kept it open. Since then, as the " Daily News "
has this month observed with equal beauty and
truth, " our history has been written in blood ";
and the beneficent work of confiscation and disestablishment at home has been stayed.

CHAPTER I.

THE COMPETENCE OF RADICAL POLITICIANS TO DEAL WITH FOREIGN AFFAIRS.

"PERICLES, the great Athenian statesman, said with regard to women, their greatest merit was to be never heard of. Now what Pericles untruly said of women, I am very much disposed to say of Foreign Affairs—their great merit would be to be never heard of."

> In Mr. Gladstone's Speech at West Calder, 27th Nov. 1879.

It is interesting to compare with the above words the following :—

"Mr. Gladstone evidently forgets that Foreign Affairs are simply the affairs of this country in foreign parts."

> Mr. Disraeli, during General Election of 1874.

And

"Nothing could be foreign to us."

> Mr. Cowen, in his speech at Newcastle, 31st Jan. 1880.

[9]

The true character of Russia.

"I do not believe the Emperor of Russia is a man of aggressive schemes of policy. I have no fear myself of the territorial extensions of Russia in Asia—no fear of them whatever. I think such fears are only old women's fears."

Gladstone, 27th Nov. 1879.

"The chronic fear of Russia arises from a long-held suspicion based upon a profound ignorance of all the facts of the case."

"One of the two causes why war was avoided last year was the moderation of Russia immediately after her triumph over Turkey."

"If Russia and England were as friendly as Russia always wished to be."

Three extracts from Mr. Bright's speech at Birmingham in the "Times" of 18th March 1879.

"Russia is the refuge of the afflicted, the protector of the unprotected, and the father of the fatherless."

Mr. Lowe, at Croydon, in the "Times" of 14th Sept. 1876.

The Ameer of Afghanistan at this time had evidently formed an erroneous estimate of Russia's character, for one of his reasons in declining an English Mission was that a "pretext might thereby be afforded to the Russians for deputing a similar mission to Cabul; that the circumstance of their having given assurances to the contrary would not stop them; that the Russians broke treaties at pleasure, were very pushing in their policy, and feared no one ; that the recent history of Europe showed that the English were unable to compel the Russians to adhere to treaties, and were equally impotent to arrest Russian aggression."

Perhaps he had been scared by the bogey of Peter the Great's Will, which contains the following advice :—

" Approach as near as possible to Constantinople and towards the Indies.   He who reigns at Constantinople will be the real sovereign of the world, and with that object in view, provoke continual wars with Turkey and with Persia; establish dockyards in the Black sea ; get possession of the shores of that sea as well as those of the Baltic, these two things being necessary for the ultimate success of our project; hasten the decadency of Persia; penetrate as far as the Persian Gulf ; re-establish the former trade of the Levant by appropriating Syria; and, if possible, extend the power of Russia to the Indies, which are the emporium of the world."

Nor does Mr. Cowen agree with Mr. Lowe, for he describes Russia as a—

> " Crushing and devouring despotism, which annihilated full fifty nationalities."

Their knowledge.

> " I know nothing of scientific military frontiers."

> Mr. Childers, in the " Times" of 28th Nov. 1878.

"It has always been said by our opponents that if Russia held a strong position at Merv —and I do not affirm or deny the statement, *for I have no particular information on the point*—that it would mean a most formidable state of things for British India. But so long as the late Government was in office there was no talk about Russia in Merv."

> Mr. Gladstone. Speech in Buckinghamshire, in the "Times" of 23rd April 1879.

It does not seem to have occurred to Mr. Gladstone that there was no talk about Russia in Merv, because Russia was not there or near there.

The occupation of Constantinople by the Russians is a matter of indifference to us, for, in Mr. Chamberlain's words in the "Times" of 1st May 1878,—

"Was it wise for them to go into panic like old women, even if Constantinople was occupied by the Russians?"

So, Mr. Forster is of opinion

"That it is not especially our business by English troops or English money to keep Russia out of Constantinople."

> "Times," 7th Jan. 1878.

Compare with this what Mr. Cowen says:—

"If Russia obtained political supremacy on the other side of the Bosphorus, she could close the canal and intercept our way to India by the Euphrates Valley. North of the Danube she was comparatively harmless, but with the Black Sea, the Sea of Marmora, and the Straits, she would have a position unequalled in the world for commerce and for war. This position was the key to Europe, one of the life-arteries, and its occupation by a conquering ambitious power would be a danger to England, to Europe, and to liberty."

The Duke of Argyll is of opinion that the advance of Russia in Central Asia need not frighten us ; for, as he says, "the danger which is inducing the Government to commit all those crimes and follies is a danger which need not frighten the dearest old woman in this city of Leeds." See "Times" of 15th Nov. 1879.

In his pamphlet entitled "Bulgarian Horrors," at p. 39, Mr. Gladstone treats of the Rejection of the Berlin Memorandum by our Government, and of the despatch of the British fleet to Besika Bay in May 1876, and says:—

"Partisans exulted in a diplomatic victory, and in the increase of what is called our *prestige*,—the bane, in my opinion, of all upright politics."

As prestige is only what may be termed the efficient reputation of a country, the originality of his condemnation of it is remarkable. But, in his article, "Germany, France, and England," in the "Edinburgh Review" for October 1870, he had expounded this novel doctrine at some length, and explained, in accordance with it, what should be the attitude and duties of England towards Europe. And during his last Ministry he conscientiously observed this doctrine in his foreign policy.

It is a testimony to its novelty that Lord Russell, in his "Recollections," wrote:—

> "The late Government, by their foreign policy, have tarnished the national honour, injured the national interests, and lowered the national character."

He was a very old man, and could not see its moral beauty. But Prince Bismark thoroughly appreciated it. He has said that if England had spoken out plainly, the Franco-German war might have been prevented, and "England counts for nothing. England will prate a little, and say a few big words, but that is all, so long as the present Administration (*i.e.* that of Mr. Gladstone) is in power." And at that time he gave it as his opinion that England was a "finished" power.

> "You have Gibraltar, Malta; the Suez Canal, Perim, and Aden. You have all these stepping-stones to India, and you have India. But,¹ excepting the thirty young gentlemen, who find places there every year, and a profit of ten million pounds, there is not a single

result which is beneficial to the thirty-four millions of the population of the United Kingdom."

Mr. Bright, at Birmingham, in the " Times " of 17th April 1879.

So that Mr. Bright is fully as aware of the worthlessness of prestige, and refuses to admit that we derive any sentimental disadvantage of that kind from our possession of India. No mention is made of the benefits which our rule has conferred on the peoples of India. No doubt a lofty disinclination to praise his own country is the cause of this silence.

Our Colonial Resources.

In the Queen's Speech, at the close of the Session of 1878, an allusion is made to the soldiers whom Canada had been ready to send to our aid when a war with Russia was probable.

Mr. Gladstone, in " England's Mission," in the " Nineteenth Century Review " for September 1878, p. 572, with instinctive right feeling, says :—

" The vain-glorious boast which Ministers, aware that there could be no reply, have inserted in the speech of Her Majesty on the prorogation, as to aid which the Colonies would have given us in a war that might have been, can only excite ridicule,"

and,—

" Ostentatious proclamation to the world of the military aid they are to give us is much

more likely to check than to develope any dis-
position of that kind, and savours strongly of
an age of imposture."

Mr. Bright himself could not have denounced
the insolent vulgarity of this boast more vigorously.

Lord Beaconsfield, speaking at the Guildhall, on
the 9th November 1876, said that:— *Our own Resources.*

"England was not a country that, when she
enters into a campaign, has to ask herself
whether she can support a second or third
campaign. She enters into a campaign,
which she will not terminate till right is
done."

This boast, if boast it be, roused the noble indig-
nation of Mr. Lowe. He severely censured it, at a
length which forbids us from reproducing his words
here, in a speech in the "Times" of 15th November 1876. He said it ought to make every
Englishman blush to hear such a statement. And,
in truth, the occasion when it was made aggravated
its enormity tenfold. Once before, Russia had been
led into a war with England from a mistaken
estimate of the strength and determination of England. At this time Russia was not unlikely to
make a similar mistake. Determined words and
preparations for action could alone prevent it. Lord
Beaconsfield used such words. They ought to
make us blush, said Mr. Lowe.

Tories sometimes covertly hint that the Radical *The Intrepidity of the Radicals.*

party is inclined to acquiesce in Russian aggression. Can any insinuation be more groundless? Why, in December 1878 Mr. Gladstone censured the Government for not having gone to war with Russia. He said :—

"If Russia sent a mission to Cabul, why have we not called Russia to account ? "

Can it be, then, that Mr. Bright for a moment forgot that Mr. Gladstone was not in the Cabinet, when he said soon afterwards :—

"You have a Government that would lead this Christian nation into a sanguinary, murderous contest over two great continents of the globe."

Mr. Freeman's exclamation at St. James' Hall on 9th Dec. 1876, "Perish our dominion in India, rather than that we should strike a blow in such a cause as that of the Porte," was sufficiently dashing; while for calm disregard of probable and terrible consequences the following sentence of Mr. Gladstone's cannot be surpassed :—

"My purpose," he said, "has been for the last eighteen months, day and night, week by week, and month by month, to counterwork what I believe to be the purpose of Lord Beaconsfield."

At Oxford, 31st Jan. 1878.

The victorious troops of Russia were at that time camping by the walls of Constantinople. But for the fear that their entry into the city would lead to a war with England, they would at once have entered into it. It was the avowed and fixed policy of Lord Beaconsfield to keep the Russians out of Constantinople, and to treat their entry into it as a cause of war. The leader of the Radical party, who loudly boasted at that time that he spoke the voice of the majority of the nation, thus declared his persistent opposition to this policy of Lord Beaconsfield. Was it Mr. Gladstone's fault that war did not ensue ?

"I hope that if a Liberal Ministry comes by and by into office, it will have the courage to put an end to that stupid Convention which obliges us, under certain circumstances, to defend Turkey ; to give up Cyprus, or hand it over to Greece ; to withdraw from financial interference in Egypt in the interest of bondholders at the expense of the poor miserable population of that country; to abandon projects of aggression both in Asia and Africa ; and to concentrate the attention of the British people upon their own industrial progress and moral improvement." *Their future Foreign Policy.*

> Mr. Baxter, in "Times" of 26th Sept. 1879.

In the Debate on the "Royal Titles" Bill, Mr. Lowe argued that it was inexpedient to take a *Their Caution.*

territorial title from India, as we might lose our Empire there, and added :—

> " Most of us remember how very near we were losing India some twenty years ago."

Their Popularity in Russia.

> " No doubt the Russians would gladly see a change in the position of parties in England."

> > "Russia and England," by O. K., p. 278.

> " Mr. Gladstone, the only foreign statesman whom the Russians had regarded with confidence and esteem."

> " Mr. Gladstone, Mr. Bright, Mr. Freeman, the Duke of Argyll, whose names will ever be precious to us."

> > *Ibid.* p. 268.

O. K., the writer of these remarks, is a Russian lady, the sister of General Kireéff, an officer on the Staff of the Grand Duke Constantine.

The Tory Government has obstinately refused to carry out the views of foreign policy embodied in the preceding extracts. It has, on the contrary, clung with superstitious devotion to the traditional policy of Great Britain ; its selfish aim has been to maintain her honour and interests. Moreover, it has been successful, and has thus committed that which, in the case of Tories, is the one unpardonable offence. Were Radicals to assist the Government in carrying out this policy, or even to look tranquilly on its execution ? Good heavens ! no. It is the bounden duty of all good Radicals at all times, and under all circumstances, to thwart a Tory policy and vilify Tory statesmen. The following gems will give a feeble idea of the gusto with which they have fulfilled this duty.

" The honour of the British name, which in the deplorable events of the year has been more gravely compromised than I have known it to be at any former period." *Their powers of Abuse.*

> Mr. Gladstone in " Bulgarian Horrors," pp. 49 and 50.

" The crimes, the follies, the cruelties of the Government."

> Sir W. Lawson in the " Times " of 18th Oct. 1878.

" The Government can never open its lips without making statements full of the most gross inaccuracies. . . . The Afghan War was entirely due to the violence and the deceit of the British Government."

> Duke of Argyll in the " Times " of 15th November 1879.

" The policy of the Government was a wicked one."

> Mr. Chamberlain in the " Times " of 17th April 1879.

2 *

" The invasion of Zululand has been brought about by the most treacherous and the meanest devices on our part, and the brutality and injustice of it are perfectly appalling."

Sir W. Lawson, at Cockermouth, 16th April 1879.

" The Afghan War had begun in treachery of the basest kind, and no words were strong enough to describe the atrocities that were going on there."

Sir W. Lawson, at Deerham, 16th June 1879.

" The Afghan War was the most atrocious massacring of human beings that ever was heard of."

Sir W. Lawson, at Cockermouth, 16th April 1879.

On the 2nd of December 1878 Mr. Gladstone said :—

" Our opponents, whom I like also to call our friends, for political opposition ought not to interfere with personal respect."

It will therefore, perhaps, not be considered a waste of time to see how the Radicals display their personal respect for their " friends." Their first love seems to have been Lord Derby. Of him we find Mr. Chamberlain, on the 23rd of October 1876, speaking as follows :—

" The possibility of impending war was distinctly due to the obstinate adherence of Lord Derby to the antiquated traditions of diplomacy."

Mr. Shaw Lefevre, in a speech in the "Times" of 2nd November 1876, pleasantly described him as—

> "Without any generous sympathies for anything, always ready with his blanket to extinguish any enthusiasm, and always ready with objections to any course."

And Mr. E. A. Freeman, in the "Times" of 10th October 1876, averred that—

> "The Lord Derby of 1876 was the Lord Stanley of 1866 and 1867, who, by a stroke of his pen, handed over the Christians of Crete to their Turkish tyrants."

And Mr. Mundella, with his analytical power, characterised him, in a speech in the "Times" of 3rd September 1876—

> "As a man of rather a glacial temperament, cold, and phlegmatic; his blood was very sluggish, and his sympathies were not easily excited; he always saw one thousand reasons why nothing should be done, and why everything should remain as it was."

Is it the same Mr. Mundella who, on the 13th of March 1880, said that he believed "Lord Derby would play a distinguished part in the Liberal politics of the country"?

Strange to say, in the spring of 1878, their affection for Lord Derby cooled, and they became passionately enamoured of Lord Cranbrook. Thus, we find them speaking of his despatch of the 18th November 1878, in the following terms:—

"I unhesitatingly say the narrative I have read to you is incomplete, incorrect, misleading, and disingenuous. If I were in the habit of using the Prime Minister's language, I should attach to it a still stronger epithet."

"Was there ever, in diplomatic history, a mis-statement so flagrant as that which the Government has published in the newspapers?"

Mr. Childers, "Times," 28th Nov. 1879.

Next, Lord Salisbury is described as—

" A man who has prostrated his intellect in the hope of purchasing a succession which may never come."

Mr. Bright, in the "Times" of 27th Oct. 1879.

And, again,—

" But what did Lord Salisbury do? At the very first he directed the Indian Government to practice deceit towards the Ameer."

Duke of Argyll, in the "Times" of 15th Nov. 1879.

While the " gay wisdom " of Sir W. Lawson thus described the Prime Minister :—

> " Lord Beaconsfield is ten times worse than Ahab ever was."

16th April 1879.

After this we are not surprised to find Mr. Chamberlain comparing the Cabinet to the " Long Firm "—a notorious gang of swindlers—or, finally, Mr. Bright with comprehensive charity exclaiming :—

> " And yet, Sir, there were criminals at head-quarters, and there were fools and imbeciles among the people, and there was baseness enough among the proprietors and writers of some newspapers—there was all this to give for a time a semblance of popularity to a madness and guilt such as I have described."

In the " Times " of the 27th Oct. 1879.

Well may Mr. Gladstone ask :—

> " Why has the country been flooded with controversy of a more violent, and I am sorry to say, of a more gross character than is known to the annals of our political controversy? "

In the " Times " of 31st Jan. 1878.

He forgets that,

"We are party men first and last on all questions."

Sir William Harcourt, 7th Oct. 1878.

CHAPTER II.

THE COMPETENCE OF RADICAL POLITICIANS TO DEAL WITH DOMESTIC AFFAIRS.

"The interests we have harassed I would harass still."

Their Policy in the Future.

> Mr. Lowe in the "Times" of 5th Nov. 1879.

This is pleasant intelligence for officers in the Army and Navy, Civil Servants, Dockyard Labourers, Licensed Victuallers, Clergy of Churches to be disestablished, owners of lands to be confiscated, beneficiaries of endowments,—in a word, for the community at large.

"When the time comes, as I have said it may come, that Scotch opinion shall be fully formed upon the subject" (*i.e.* Disestablishment of the Scotch Church) "the Liberal party in England will do its best to give effect to that Scotch opinion, without undue consideration

Their Capacity to lead the Nation.

being given to any other circumstances con-
nected with the question."

Lord Hartington, at Edinburgh, in
the " Times " of 7th Nov. 1877.

The meaning of which is, that when it is clear
that a majority of the Scotch electors are in favour
of either retaining or disestablishing their State
Church, the Liberal party will eagerly carry out
their manifest desires. And this it will do, whether it is in favour of such a course or not, and
with a thorough disregard of whether such a course
will be favourable or unfavourable to the State
Church of England. It is only provoking that
the complaisance of the Liberal party should not
more quickly lead to a decisive expression of opinion on the part of the Scotch Electors, so that
Lord Hartington might be able to carry out at
once what Lord Derby has called "the instructions
of his employers."

" I, Gentlemen, have very little to say upon
the question of the Disestablishment of the
Church at this moment, because you are sub-
stantially in possession of my opinions. The
opinion I have indicated is perfectly trans-
parent. I do not think it is a question for
me to determine, so much as it is for the
people of Scotland."

Mr. Gladstone at Dalkeith, 26th
Nov. 1879.

A truly marvellous instance of self-restraint. For Mr. Gladstone must have had a great deal to say on this question. His book on the connection between Church and State was his first contribution to political knowledge ; his Disestablishment of the Irish Church is his most destructive piece of legislation. He is not unfamiliar with the religious controversies of Scotland. He must, then, have made up his mind and come to the conclusion that the Disestablishment of the Scotch Church would be either beneficial or injurious to Scotland. Yet, without a word of impertinent advice, such as statesmen have heretofore given on such grave matters, he leaves the question to the unaided judgments of the " people of Scotland."

In 1865 Mr. Gladstone said that the Disestablishment of the Irish Church was not a question of practical politics. In 1868 he proposed Resolutions to the House of Commons in favour of its Disestablishment. What brought the question into the range of practical politics? He has very candidly told us this himself:— Practical Hints to Agitators.

> " When it came to this—that a great jail in the heart of the Metropolis was broken open under circumstances which drew the attention of the English people to the state of Ireland, and when in Manchester policemen were murdered in the execution of their duty, at once the whole country became alive to Irish questions; and the question

of the Irish Church revived. It came within the range of practical politics. I myself took it up, and proposed Resolutions to the House of Commons declaring that the Irish Church ought no longer to exist as an Establishment."

> In Mr. Gladstone's speech at Dalkeith, 26th Nov. 1879.

Encouragement to Confiscators. Proposals have been made to cut up the land of the United Kingdom into a multitude of small properties. Far be it from Mr. Gladstone to discourage their authors, for,

> " To a proposal of that kind, I for one am not going to object upon the ground that it would be inconsistent with the privileges of landed proprietors. . . . The State is perfectly entitled, if it please, to buy out the landed proprietors as it may think fit for the purpose of dividing the property into small lots."

> In Mr. Gladstone's speech at Dalkelth, 26th Nov. 1879.

> " There is no democrat, there is no agitator, there is no propounder of anti-rent doctrines, whatever mischief he may do, who can compare in mischief with Her Majesty's Government."

> In Mr. Gladstone's speech at Glasgow, 5th Dec. 1879.

Writing in the " Nineteenth Century " for August 1879, p. 206, he declares :— Mr. Gladstone and Obstruction.

> " It is too true, indeed, that the House of Commons is fast becoming incapable of the due and sufficient discharge of its functions. If those who have had the main share in bringing about this state of things are mainly to bear the brand of obstruction, then, I apprehend, there is no doubt that at this hour the chief obstructionists are the Government."

> " It is thus recognised that nearness (to the seat of government) is a reason for having a more limited number of members, and consequently that distance from the seat of government constitutes a claim for a larger number of members than the population warrants." A new Principle of Representation.
>
> In Mr. Gladstone's speech at Dalkeith, 26th Nov. 1879.

We cannot helf suspecting that the statement that this principle was a " recognised " one, is a fine example of Mr. Gladstone's modesty. Surely, this principle is not recognised, and never had been dreamed of until it entered into his receptive brain. But when once stated it has the simple cogency of all great truths. Of course, populations furthest from the seat of government ought to have the most members, for in all probability they know less about the course of events than those nearer to London. They are, too, further removed from the corrupting influence of the educated classes and the clever metropolitan press. How well, moreover, the principle would work. It would enable Scotland to return so many more safe and silent Radicals. How eagerly will the dwellers in Paris and Rome accept this novel dogma!

Their Love
f Country.

"But while we have been advancing with this portentous rapidity, America is passing us by in a canter."

> Mr. Gladstone's "Kin Beyond Sea," in the "North American Review."

"With us America is always understood to mean North America, and rather especially the United States, than the portion of it which is still dependent upon the British Crown."

> Mr. Bright, at Rochdale.

"The United States would make fifteen times France, it would made twelve times Germany, and it would make twenty-five times Great Britain and Ireland. That is an astounding fact . . . We have colonies, vast possessions in Canada, in Australia, in India, and in South Africa, where nobody yet knows how much. But you must remember that all these territories in Canada, in Australia, in India, and in South Africa are neither in men nor in money in the way of revenue any strength to the people in the United Kingdom. On the contrary they are continually drawing from our resources."

" There is no doubt there is a great difference between the United States and these in Europe, with the exception of one great country, and that is France. I believe what he (Mr. Potter) says that he only saw four drunken people in America. Well, but he saw no Emperor. He did not see an Emperor or an Empress, or Kings or Queens, or Imperial or Royal Princes or Princesses. Those great dignitaries to whom we pay so great, and often so deserved, respect are not to be found in that country."

At Rochdale, in the " Times " of 19th
Sept. 1879.

What could Lord Palmerston have meant when he said that he would never offer office to Mr. Bright because " he had not the slightest feeling of an Englishman about him ? "

" We have, in point of fact, not one single measure to point to which has been the result of the deliberations of the present Administration."

Domestic Policy of the Present Government.

Mr. Bright, at Birmingham, in the
" Times " of 17th April 1879.

" There is no domestic policy in this country now. Under the auspices of the present Administration domestic legislation and the care of our own people have well-nigh ceased to exist."

> Sir W. Harcourt, at Oxford, in the "Times" of 15th Jan. 1879.

Yet the present Administration has introduced social reforms into every part of English society, by the following Acts :—

The Factory and Workshop,
   Public Health,
   Pollution of Rivers,
   Artisans and Labourers' Dwellings,
   Friendly Societies,
   Employers and Workmen,
   Agricultural Holdings,
   Contagious Diseases (Animals),
   Intermediate Education ⎫ in Ireland,
   University Education ⎭
   Unseaworthy Ships,
   Army Discipline,
   English Universities,
   Prisons, and
   Relief of Distress in Ireland Acts,
            &c. &c. &c.

And has now in hand—
   Criminal Code,
   Bankruptcy,
   Reform of the Land Laws Bills,
      and other useful measures.

Superficial readers may find it difficult at first to reconcile the Radical statements with this list of actual Tory measures. But the explanation of this merely apparent inconsistency is obvious. These measures have provoked no bitter opposition, and excited no class or sectarian jealousies. They have injured no profession—no trade. They have merely done good in a quiet way. They have inflicted no wrongs in a violent way. Therefore, of course, they do not represent a domestic policy. A domestic policy, to be worthy of its name, must necessarily involve the destruction of some institution, the confiscation of some property, or a diminution of the rights, and an interference with the interests, of some church, class, or trade. It must be drastic ; it must be opposed to the desires of a large portion of the electors ; its merit rises in proportion to its violence and to its unpopularity; and if only a casual combination of Welsh, Scotch, and Irish voters can swamp the votes of an enthusiastic majority of the people of England, and force a measure, which affects England alone, upon an indignant England,—that, indeed, is heroic legislation, and its author, in truth, an inspired statesmen.

CHAPTER III.

The Political Foresight of Radicals.

" All politics consist in a foresight of what is likely to occur, and he who foresees most truly is the best politician."

> Sir W. Harcourt, in the " Times " of 3rd Oct. 1879.

" Trade is most nearly affected by foreign politics ; and the Government have so dis- turbed foreign politics that trade has but little chance of revival."

> Sir W. Harcourt, in 1879.

Sir W. Harcourt notwithstanding, the Board of Trade Returns for the months of January and February 1880 conclusively show that trade has revived. The following is the value of the exports and imports of those two months, as compared with a similar period in the years 1878 and 1879.

	1880.	1879.	1878.
Exports	33,417,000 ;	26,909,000 ;	30,320,000
Imports	65,618,000 ;	55,028,000 ;	62,785,000

Moreover, the London Clearing House returns show that the bills and cheques cleared during the week ending the 12th of March last, amounted to £94,232,000, being an increase upon the corresponding period of last year of £16,672,000.

The same seer has also spoken as follows :

"It cannot be, indeed, it is not disputed, that the Indian revenue is inadequate to its expenditure. The delusion that India is a wealthy country of boundless resources is for ever dispelled. Triumphing over the infirmities of nature by his almost unexampled efforts, Mr. Fawcett has exposed the delusiveness of Indian budgets."

On the 22nd of February 1880, Sir J. Strachey announced that the Indian Government, after paying £3,200,000 towards the expenses of the Afghan War, and £1,670,000 for frontier railways, had a surplus of £119,000.

"I will only say that it is she (America) alone who, at a coming time, can, and probably will, wrest from us that commercial

supremacy. We have no title ; I have no
inclination to murmur at this prospect. If
she acquires it, she will make the acquisition
by the right of the strongest ; but in this
instance the strongest means the best. She
will, probably, become what we are now, the
head servant in the great household of the
world, the employer of all employed ; because
her service will be the most and ablest. We
have no more title against her than Venice,
or Genoa, or Holland, has had against us."

> From "Kin beyond Sea," an article
> by Mr. Gladstone, appropriately
> published in the "North Ame-
> rican Review."

Mr. Mundella, in a speech in the "Times" of
31st August 1876, said :—

> Mr. Disraeli had effaced himself by taking
> another name. . . ."

And, in a speech at Sheffield, in the "Times" of
5th September 1876 :—

> "He believed the end was drawing nigh,
> and that Mr. Disraeli's elevation to the Peer-
> age was but the prelude to the decline and
> fall of that invertebrate Toryism which had
> been so injurious to the best interests of the
> country."

But Lord Beaconsfield and Toryism, "invertebrate," or otherwise, still, alas! survive.

Sir W. Harcourt, in his speech at Oxford, in the " Times " of 13th January 1879, said:—

> " Suppose the Roumelians have an unconquerable aversion to the form of government which Lord Beaconsfield has so kindly provided for them, what will happen then ? They may resist, and then you will have another Servian or Bulgarian war, with all the amenities which belong to the hostilities of those climes."

Unfulfilled.

> " The Eastern Roumelia of Berlin is just one of those ingenious pieces of political clockwork, which have every merit except that they will not go."

Proved to be false: the " clock-work " has gone and is going.

> " I do not believe the Treaty of Berlin to be a settlement of peace . . . . . They have given to this people a peace which is no peace."

As yet, shown to be false.

> " We frame a constitution to satisfy the population, and then we find we must send an army to cram it down their throats. '

Sir W. Harcourt was here alluding to the joint military occupation of Eastern Roumelia, which he then thought would be necessary.

This has been proved to be false.

> "I do not wonder that the Government should shrink from the name of a dissolution with which they were once so fond of menacing us. No, sir, they will not dissolve, but they will be dissolved."

Proved to be false.

Sir W. Harcourt, in his speech at Sheffield, in the "Times" of 17th April 1879:—

> "Everyone knows that the Treaty of Berlin is unworkable, and that something else must be devised to take its place . . . the Treaty of Berlin has failed, and will fail.

Not fulfilled as yet.

> "And so, I suppose, the conflict of races (in Roumelia) is to begin in about a fortnight hence."

It did not, and has not yet begun.

As Sir William Harcourt's predictions and jests are of the same quality, it is not really incongruous to quote here the following sentence, which is reported to be his most refined effort of humour:—

> "The system of the present Government which has brought us nothing but danger,

debt, disaster, distrust, disquiet, and distress."
(Loud laughter and cheers.)

> In Sir W. Harcourt's speech at
> Sheffield, in the "Times" of
> 17th April 1879.

In the next jest it will be observed that Sir W.
Lawson has not quite an equal command of allite-
rative words; but it is a praiseworthy attempt:—

> "The policy of the Government is a policy
> of blood and bluster, brag and bounce."
> (Much laughter and cheers.)

> Sir W. Lawson.

Poor Mr. Disraeli, who has no sense of humour.
actually said, in a debate on the Reform Bill of
1860:—

> "Alliteration tickles the ear, and is a very
> popular form of language among savages."

CONCLUSION.

THE foregoing extracts, to some extent, show the zeal and ability with which the most conspicuous Radicals have, by words, laboured to accomplish that which is the highest aim of modern Radicalism —the discomfiture of their English opponents. But in order to appreciate fully their efforts to achieve this end, it is necessary to allude to the general course of their arguments and to their acts.

When the invasion of Turkey by Russia took place, an overwhelming majority of Englishmen of all parties, were resolved to support the Government in defending certain clearly defined English and European interests against the aggression of Russia. It was plain that Russia would in all probability attack these interests, if she thought that she could do so with impunity. It was plain that she would not attack them, if she was persuaded that England was, as a nation, willing and prepared to fight in their defence. The Radical politicians must have been aware of both these facts. Our Government proposed successive measures of military preparation, which were clearly necessary to secure these interests against attack, and so to preserve the peace of Europe. Yet these Radicals deliberately and bitterly opposed the adoption of each one of these measures, loudly boasting on each occasion that now they had the nation at their back. They opposed the vote for the £6,000,000, and were beaten by 328 votes to 120; they opposed the calling out of the Reserves, and were beaten by 310 votes to 64. In a minority of 126, they protested against the despatch of the Indian troops to Malta, as against a majority of 226; and they sought to censure the Anglo-Turkish Convention, and were defeated by 338 votes to 195. All, therefore, that they could do, by open opposition in Parliament, they did, to embarrass the Government, and to make the enemies of European peace think that the Government was not supported by the nation. Nay, they did more. With the same lofty ambition to embarrass the Tories, they have studiously, from time to time, consciously or unconsciously, misrepresented the question at issue, and, in effect, deceived a portion of the English people. Thus, from the outbreak of the insurrection in the Herzegovina to the Treaty of Berlin, they persistently maintained that the Eastern Question was the question simply of the condition of the Christian subjects of the Porte. During that time they maintained that Russia was an unselfish and beneficent Power, and ignored or denied the interests of Great Britain in the distribution of power in the south-east of Europe and Asia Minor. By these contentions they unquestionably encouraged, if they did not enable, Russia to fight the War with Turkey. At the conclusion of the War these Radicals, in their anxiety that harsh terms should be imposed upon Turkey, were content that the Treaty should be dictated by Russia to Turkey, and discouraged the interference of Europe in the settlement of its terms. Incidentally, they thereby did what they could to weaken the binding force of existing treaties, and to discredit the .concer: of the Great Powers.

In reference to the Central Asian policy of our Government, they have hardly ever mentioned the encroachments of Russia in those regions. To have done so might have helped rather than have injured the Government of their country. And this reflection helps us to realise how completely these Radicals have given themselves up to the one task of discrediting the Tory Government. What it did might be right and patriotic: what matter? The Government that did it was Tory. In their execution of this task they have risen superior to obsolete notions of patriotism, and cast off all narrow prejudices in favour of their country and their fellow-countrymen. There is no savage tribe, no nationality, which is being forced into an artificial life, of whose supposed interests they have not been more careful than of the historic fame of Great Britain. To the members of her Government they have persistently attributed motiveless greed, purposeless cruelty, gratuitous mendacity. On no occasion have they made allowance for its manifold difficulties; on no occasion, until after the elections at Liverpool and Southwark, have they cordially helped to remove them. They have evinced a malicious zeal in attacking servants of the Crown in all parts of the world, who have been simply executing, amidst aggravated difficulties, the policy of the Queen. And not a few of them have displayed an astonishing alacrity to impugn the humanity of English officers in the field, and have been more eager to accuse English soldiers, while engaged in war, of some crime or weakness, than to recognise their bravery and their discipline.

By these courses of conduct the Radicals have, without doubt, from time to time weakened the influence of England throughout the world, and impaired the vigour of her policy. Shall we now reward this conduct by surrendering into their hands the government of the British Empire?

AFGHANISTAN, AND THE CENTRAL ASIAN QUESTION, &c.

Selected from **W. H. ALLEN & CO.'s** *Catalogue.*

HERAT: The Granary and Garden of Central Asia.

With an Index and a Map. By Colonel G. B. MALLESON, C.S.I., Author of "History of the Indian Mutiny." 8vo. 8s.

"Colonel Malleson's book on Herat is full of valuable information, and deserves the fullest attention of everyone interested in Central Asian politics."—*Professor Vambery to "The Times."*

THE AFGHAN WAR. Gough's Action at Futteh-

abad. By the Rev. C. SWINNERTON, Bengal Chaplain, Chaplain in the Field with the First Division, Peshawur Valley Field Force. Crown 8vo., with Frontispiece and Plans, 5s.

"A spirited and accurate account of the action, compiled from descriptions furnished by the officers who were actually engaged."—*Broad Arrow.*

CENTRAL ASIAN PORTRAITS: The Celebrities

of the Khanates and the Neighbouring States. By DEMETRIUS CHARLES BOULGER, M.R.A.S., Author of "England and Russia in Central Asia." Crown 8vo. 7s. 6d.

"This is a volume as interesting as it is useful, and which ought to be studied by everyone who wishes to judge accurately of the momentous Central Asian Question."—*Whitehall Review.*

ENGLAND AND RUSSIA IN CENTRAL ASIA.

By DEMETRIUS CHARLES BOULGER, M.R.A.S., Author of "The Life of Yakoob Beg, of Kashgar." With Appendices and two Maps, one Map being the latest Russian Official Map of Central Asia. Two vols. 8vo. 36s.

"Mr. Boulger's volumes contain an immense amount of valuable information in regard to what is known as the Central Asian Question."—*Pall Mall Gazette.*

NARRATIVE OF A JOURNEY THROUGH THE

PROVINCE OF KHORASSAN AND ON THE N.W. FRONTIER OF AFGHANISTAN IN 1875. By Colonel C. M. MACGREGOR, C.S.I., C.I.E., Bengal Staff Corps. Two vols. 8vo. With Map and numerous Illustrations. 30s.

"Exceedingly interesting, and must prove of great practical value to intending travellers in Persia. We close with regret such an entertaining book of travel; one written in a simple, unpretentious style, and yet replete with useful information."—*Army and Navy Gazette.*

THE RUSSIAN ARMY AND ITS CAMPAIGNS

IN TURKEY IN 1877–78. By F. V. GREENE, First Lieutenant in the Corps of Engineers, United States Army, and lately Military Attaché to the United States Legation at St. Petersburg. Royal 8vo., with Atlas, 32s.

" To the general reader this work cannot fail to be of interest, but to the military student it will be simply invaluable—the book is one that should be in every Regimental Library."—*Times*.

THE KABUL INSURRECTION OF 1841–42.

(Revised and corrected from Lieut. Eyre's original Manuscript.) By Major-General Sir VINCENT EYRE, K.C.S.I., C.B. Edited by Colonel G. B. Malleson, C.S.I. Crown 8vo. With Map and Illustrations. 9s.

" The republication of this volume is well justified both by the stirring nature of its contents, and the bearing which it has on recent events."—*Daily News*.

A HISTORY OF AFGHANISTAN ; from the

Earliest Period to the outbreak of the War of 1878. By Colonel G. B. MALLESON, C.S.I. Author of "Historical Sketch of the Native States of India," "History of the Indian Mutiny," &c. Second Edition. 8vo. With Map. 18s.

" At the present time there could be no more seasonable publication. The book deserves to be thoughtfully and extensively read by everybody who desires to probe to the pith of the Indian Frontier question."—*Daily Telegraph*.

THE PUS'HTO MANUAL (the Language of the

Afghans). Comprising a concise Grammar, Exercises and Dialogues, Familiar Phrases, Proverbs, and Vocabulary. By Major H. G. RAVERTY, Bo. N.I. (Retired). Author of the " Pushto Grammar," " Dictionary," &c. Fcap. 5s.

" This book shows all the painstaking care for which Major Raverty has long been famous, and it can be used with confidence by any one wishing to learn the language of the Afghans."—*Homeward Mail*.

THE RUSSIAN OFFICIAL MAP OF CENTRAL

ASIA. Compiled in accordance with the Discoveries and Surveys of Russian Staff Officers up to the close of the year 1877. In cloth cases. 14s.

The EYE-WITNESSES' ACCOUNT of the DISASTROUS RUSSIAN CAMPAIGN against the AKHAL TEKKE TURCOMANS. By CHARLES MARVIN. With Maps, Plans, and Portraits. Demy 8vo., Price 16s.

EUROPE'S ANSWER to LORD HARTINGTON and MR. GLADSTONE. By I. S. Demy 8vo. Price 6d.

The TRUE STORY of OUR AFGHAN POLICY. An Appeal to the British Nation against Factious Misrepresentations. By an INDIAN OFFICER. *Price One Penny.*

SKETCHES of DESERT LIFE. Recollections of an Expedition in the Soudan. By B. SOLYMOS. 8vo. 15s.

LANDS of PLENTY. — BRITISH NORTH AMERICA for Health, Sport, and Profit. A book for Travellers in British North America. By E. HEPPLE HALL, Author of " The Picturesque Tourist," " Handbook of American Travel," &c. Post 8vo., with Maps. 6s.

The RUSSIAN ARMY and its CAMPAIGN in TURKEY, 1877–1878. By F. V. GREENE, First Lieutenant in the Corps of Engineers, U.S. Army, with Atlas. 32s.

The CHURCH under QUEEN ELIZABETH : a Historical Sketch. By Rev. F. G. LEE. 2 vols., post 8vo. 21s.

ALBIRUNI, the CHRONOLOGY of ANCIENT NATIONS ; an English version of the Arabic Text of the Athâru-l-Bâkiya of Al-bîrûnî. By Dr. C. E. SACHAU. Royal 8vo. 42s.

Our TRAVELS in HINDUSTAN and LADAK.
By Mrs. J. C. MURRAY AYNSLEY. 8vo. 14s.

PERSONAL NARRATIVE of EVENTS, from
1799 to 1815, with Anecdotes. By the late Vice-Admiral
WM. STANHOPE LOVELL. Second edition. Fcap. 4s.

A TEXT-BOOK of INDIAN HISTORY, with
Geographical Notes, Genealogical Tables, Examination
Questions, and Chronological, Biographical, Geographical,
and General Indexes. By the Rev. G. U. POPE, D.D.
Small 4to. 12s.

Our BURMESE WARS, and RELATIONS
with BURMA: an Abstract of Military, Political, and
Commercial Operations. By Colonel W. F. B. LAURIE.
8vo. 16s. With Map and Plans.

NEARLY READY.

A CHART of FAMILY INHERITANCE ac-
cording to Orthodox MUHAMMADAN LAW. En-
larged and third edition. By A. RUMSEY, of Lincoln's
Inn.

IN THE PRESS.

NIPAL: its People, Religion, Customs, Zoology,
Botany, &c.

www.ingramcontent.com/pod-product-compliance
Lightning Source LLC
Chambersburg PA
CBHW021554270326
41931CB00009B/1210